PRESS
TOWARD
THE
MARK

A BIBLE STUDY

KATHY JOHNSTON

NAVPRESS

BRINGING TRUTH TO LIFE

P.O. Box 35001, Colorado Springs, Colorado 80935

OUR GUARANTEE TO YOU

We believe so strongly in the message of our books that we are making this quality guarantee to you. If for any reason you are disappointed with the content of this book, return the title page to us with your name and address and we will refund to you the list price of the book. To help us serve you better, please briefly describe why you were disappointed. Mail your refund request to: NavPress, P.O. Box 35002, Colorado Springs, CO 80935.

The Navigators is an international Christian organization. Our mission is to reach, disciple, and equip people to know Christ and to make Him known through successive generations. We envision multitudes of diverse people in the United States and every other nation who have a passionate love for Christ, live a lifestyle of sharing Christ's love, and multiply spiritual laborers among those without Christ.

NavPress is the publishing ministry of The Navigators. NavPress publications help believers learn biblical truth and apply what they learn to their lives and ministries. Our mission is to stimulate spiritual formation among our readers.

www.navpress.com

ISBN 1-57683-308-9

Cover design and cover photography by Steve Eames
Creative Team: Melissa Munro, Karen Lee-Thorp, Amy Spencer, Glynese Northam

Some of the anecdotal illustrations in this book are true to life and are included with the permission of the persons involved. All other illustrations are composites of real situations, and any resemblance to people living or dead is coincidental.

Unless otherwise identified, all Scripture quotations in this publication are taken from the HOLY BIBLE: NEW INTERNATIONAL VERSION® (NIV®). Copyright © 1973, 1978, 1984 by International Bible Society. Used by permission of Zondervan Publishing House. All rights reserved. Other versions used include the *New American Standard Bible* (NASB), © The Lockman Foundation 1960, 1962, 1963, 1968, 1971, 1972, 1973, 1975, 1977; *The Message: New Testament with Psalms and Proverbs* (MSG) by Eugene H. Peterson, copyright © 1993, 1994, 1995, used by permission of NavPress Publishing Group; and the *New Revised Standard Version* (NRSV), copyright © 1989, by the Division of Christian Education of the National Council of the Churches of Christ in the USA, used by permission, all rights reserved.

Printed in the United States of America

1 2 3 4 5 6 7 8 9 10 / 06 05 04 03 02

Contents

What This Study Can Do for You

Christianity is not a spectator sport. Scripture compares a persevering follower of Christ to a marathon runner—and rightly so. I identify with the analogy because God has given me a love for sports that was nurtured in my childhood and has deepened through the years. By His grace, I hope to be on the tennis courts when I'm eighty. Involvement in athletic activities has not only enhanced my abilities, it also has taught me valuable lessons about walking with God.

Enthusiasm for sports is not a prerequisite for you to benefit from this book. If you lack purpose for your life or need motivation to pursue God, if you struggle with obedience or the spiritual disciplines, if you feel alone or confused or weary, then maybe taking the time to "live in the tennis shoes of an athlete" through the twelve sessions in this book will help you.

The key ingredient for success in implementing the truths in *Press Toward the Mark* is abiding in Christ. It's possible to be goal oriented and demonstrate characteristics like zeal, discipline, and perseverance in your own strength. But rather than experiencing contentment, you may feel restless and empty. Why? Jesus points out in John 15:5 that "apart from me you can do nothing." It's only through His power that you and I can exhibit the qualities discussed in this book in a way that bears fruit for Him and produces personal satisfaction.

Whether you're a business professional, a homemaker, or a student, I pray that the truths you embrace as you compare the athlete to the vibrant Christian will inspire you to press toward the mark—to scale beyond the daily-life mentality to a heavenly perspective that breeds a passion for God.

Suggestions for Using This Study

You can use this study individually, in a small-group discussion, with a friend you are mentoring, or even as curriculum for a youth or adult Sunday school class. Immediately under each of the session titles is a key verse from the New International Version that will stimulate your thinking on the topic to be studied. You may memorize it if you wish, and you also have the option to do a verse analysis of that verse at the end of the session. (For more on how to do a verse analysis, see the appendix.)

A story from an athlete's life introduces each session. Many of these people are believers; some are not. But each of their stories will help you understand how the action they displayed, which brought success in the sports realm, is vital for the Christian as well.

Most of the questions direct you to a Bible text as a basis for your answer. Let God's Word speak to you personally. In many cases, there is no right or wrong response. For the first question of every session, you may find it helpful to use a dictionary to look up definitions. Even though some questions don't direct you to specific verses, they are intended to help you think through what it means to apply biblical truth.

Approach each session with a desire to grasp the truths learned by the athlete and to use these principles in the spiritual realm of your own life. As you begin each study with prayer, rely on the Holy Spirit to give you understanding (James 1:5) and to speak to you about how you can apply what you learn to your life (James 1:22).

The appendix explains how to do the optional verse analysis Bible study. The method you use for the twelve verses covered in this book will prove to be an invaluable tool in the future as you learn how to dig into the Bible on your own. You can use this same method to examine any passage you want to study.

Go for It

MOTIVATION TO ENTER GOD'S RACE

*Therefore since we are surrounded by such a great
cloud of witnesses, let us throw off everything that hinders
and the sin that so easily entangles, and let us run with
perseverance the race marked out for us.*
Hebrews 12:1

Life had dealt Wilma Rudolph some hard blows. Her premature birth left her vulnerable to double pneumonia and scarlet fever. An attack of polio crippled not only her leg, but also her hope of ever walking normally again. Still she dreamed of becoming a world-class athlete. Her dream motivated her to overcome all obstacles—not just to walk without a clumsy metal brace, but also to undergo grueling training that eventually earned her a spot in the 1960 Olympics. Wilma made a choice—one that involved her total commitment. This inner resolve helped her become the first woman athlete to win three track and field gold medals.[1]

Lorraine Borman, a figure-skating coach for several gold medalists, expressed what it takes to get to the Olympics: "Above all, an athlete has to make a total commitment. I've had lots of skaters who had complete physical talent, but who didn't make the mental effort. They wouldn't make it!"[2]

Just as Wilma displayed unusual determination motivated by her dream, so we as Christians must make a conscious choice to rise above mediocrity and become more than pew-sitters.

Following Christ involves paying a price, but Scripture teaches that it's even more costly to remain aloof because "those who try to make their life secure will lose it" (Luke 17:33, NRSV). Christianity is not a spectator sport! God Himself will give us the motivation we need to "run with perseverance the race marked out for us" (Hebrews 12:1).

1. Look up *motivation* in a dictionary and write a short definition in your own words.

2. What would motivate an athlete to run a race, join a league, or enter a tournament?

3. If your interests lie in art, music, crafts, cars, computers, or other areas, what has motivated you to get involved in these areas?

4. Gordon Thiessen wrote, "Coaches point out that the difference between the star and the superstar is not talent, but motivation. One is willing to pay the price and the other isn't."[3] Do you think this is true in the Christian life? Explain.

5. Christ challenged His followers to deny themselves and take up their cross (Mark 8:34). What do you think He meant when He told them to deny themselves?
   a. Ignore their own longings and cater to the demands of others.
   b. Ignore their own needs and tolerate any harsh treatment that God allows into their lives.
   c. Govern and limit their own desires so they'll have time and energy for God's agenda.
   d. Other:

6. What do you think Christ meant when He told them to take up their cross?
   a. Never protest bad treatment.
   b. Be willing to die for what they believe in.
   c. Pursue the spreading of God's truth, even if others respond with violence.
   d. Other:

7. What would it look like for you to deny yourself and take up your cross this week?

Some of us may be on Christ's team, but we're still on the bench. If we think we're just second-string, normal, everyday nobodies with not much to offer, the author of *Fit for Life* has advice for us:

> The fact of the matter is, God rarely chooses "winners" to do his work. In fact, he seems to choose the more unlikely people available: a dried up old man and a woman past menopause

to start a new nation (Genesis 18), an untrained shepherd boy to take on the champion of the Philistine army (1 Samuel 17), and a timid, young virgin to give birth to the Savior of the world (Matthew 1). God doesn't require talent, strength, good looks, popularity. All he requires is a willing heart.[4]

8. How do you respond to the above quotation? (Does it encourage you? Seem irrelevant to you? ...)

9. Motivations for us to commit our lives to God are listed in the chart below. Look up the passages and complete the chart.

PASSAGE/MOTIVATION	HOW CAN THIS MOTIVATE US?
Romans 12:1 Mercies of God	
1 Corinthians 6:19-20 Our bodies belong to God	
1 Corinthians 9:24-25 Eternal rewards	
2 Corinthians 5:14-15 Christ's love	

10. Grace motivated and empowered the apostle Paul to become all he could be for God. Look up 1 Corinthians 15:9-10 and write it in your own words.

11. Maybe you don't feel ready to go all out for God. If you don't, write or talk about what leads you to prefer a slower pace.

APPLICATION
Grace is the root from which gratitude grows. When we grasp all that God has done for us, our hearts respond freely. Running the race is not something we "have to do." It becomes the desire of our heart! Hebrews 12:1 encourages us to throw off weights that may hinder us. Are there areas in your life that you want to lay aside so you can run the race better? Explain.

OPTIONAL ASSIGNMENT
Use the space below to complete a Verse Analysis Bible Study of the key verse for this session. Detailed instructions on how to do verse analysis are found in the appendix.

Hebrews 12:1
A. Read the **context before** and summarize it (Hebrews 11).

B. Read the **context after** and summarize it (Hebrews 12:2-3).

C. **Paraphrase** the verse.

D. Write out **questions** or problems you may have from this passage.
   1.

   2.

   3.

   4.

E. Look up and comment on **cross references** that give you further insight on this passage.
   1.

   2.

   3.

   4.

F. What **application** would you like to make from this study?

Give It All You've Got

ZEAL TO EXCEL FOR GOD

Do you not know that in a race all the runners run, but only one gets the prize? Run in such a way as to get the prize.

1 Corinthians 9:24

What a difference between an athlete who goes through the motions and one with a heart to win! In 1990 at the age of 43, Nolan Ryan hurled a no-hitter—he was the oldest man to achieve such a feat. Despite nagging back pain, he gave it all he had and became the only major league player to pitch no-hit games in three separate decades.[1] Baseball isn't the only arena where whole-hearted effort stands out. In the church setting there's a vast distinction between a bland believer and one with a passion for God!

Zeal to excel for the Lord isn't something we can muster up—it comes from God Himself. Mike Singletary, a former Chicago Bears linebacker, said, "My *intensity* as an athlete, husband, and father basically boils down to this: God's grace . . . what He has done for me."[2] Because both Ryan and Singletary were believers, they were able to draw on God's resources for their athletic feats and personal pursuits.

In ancient Greece a great sports spectacle called the Isthmian Games was held in Corinth every two years. It was probably this event, as well as a sense of God's overwhelming grace in his own life, that moved the apostle Paul to describe his own life quest like this: "You've all been to the stadium and seen the athletic race. Everyone runs; one wins. Run to win. All good athletes train hard.

They do it for a gold medal that tarnishes and fades. You're after one that's gold eternally. I don't know about you, but I'm running hard for the finish line. I'm giving it everything I've got. No sloppy living for me" (1 Corinthians 9:24-26, MSG).

1. Look up *zeal* in a dictionary and define it.

2. Restate Colossians 3:23 in your own words.

3. Not all of us win trophies, but deep down we know when we're trying as hard as we can. Share about a time during a sports event, music contest, business venture, or other experience when you felt you gave your best effort.

4. In which areas of your life do you find it hard to be wholehearted?

5. An NHL hockey player named Mike Gartner said, "As long as I can look in the mirror and say, 'I've done my best with the talent the Lord has given me,' then I can say I've been successful."[3] List a few abilities God has given you, and rate how much you are using each. Use a scale from 1 (minimal use) to 10 (optimal use).

6. Choose one of the abilities you listed above. Describe what it would look like for you to be using this skill to its full potential.

7. What would it take for you to get there?

8. Romans 12:11 says, "Never be lacking in zeal, but keep your spiritual fervor, serving the Lord." Name one or two biblical characters or contemporary people and tell how they've displayed zeal for God.

9. In Philippians 3:12, what do you think Paul means when he says he wants to "press on to take hold of that for which Christ Jesus took hold of me"? What does pressing on look like?

10. God wants us to live for Him "with all our heart." Read the verses and complete the chart.

PASSAGE/ WHOLEHEARTED ACTIVITY	HOW I CAN DEMONSTRATE THIS
Deuteronomy 6:5 Love God	
Deuteronomy 10:12 Serve God	
2 Kings 23:3 Obey God	
Proverbs 3:5 Trust God	
Jeremiah 29:13 Seek God	

APPLICATION

First Corinthians 9:24 urges us to strive to win the prize. Philippians 4:13 assures us that we can do all things through Christ who'll strengthen us. Write or share how, with God's help, you can be more wholehearted in running your "race" this week.

OPTIONAL ASSIGNMENT

Use the space on the following page to complete a Verse Analysis Bible Study of the key verse for this session. Detailed instructions on how to do this study are found in the appendix.

1 Corinthians 9:24

A. Read the **context before** and summarize it (1 Corinthians 9:19-23).

B. Read the **context after** and summarize it (1 Corinthians 10:1-10).

C. **Paraphrase** the passage.

D. Write out **questions** or problems you may have from this passage.
   1.

   2.

   3.

   4.

E. Look up and comment on **cross references** that give you further insight on this passage.
   1.

   2.

   3.

   4.

F. What **application** would you like to make from this study?

Listen to the Coach

SUBMISSION TO CHRIST'S AUTHORITY

*Let us fix our eyes on Jesus, the author and
perfecter of our faith.*
Hebrews 12:2

When the head coach calls the plays, the success of the game depends on each player carrying out his or her plans. Tom Osborne led the Nebraska football squad in the 1980s and 1990s to victory after victory. After a perfect season that gave them the national championship for the second year in a row, one of his players named Tyrone Williams said, "I wanted to go out and play my heart out for Coach Osborne."[1] Jeff Makovicka added, "It didn't matter who was in or at what position. Whatever it took to get the job done was our only focus."[2] Clinton Childs talked about Osborne's character on and off the field: "He stuck behind me and all of the players 100%."[3] Tom Osborne was not only a great coach but also a dedicated Christian. Because the team experienced his understanding of and commitment to them, they responded to his directives and gave everything they had in the games.[4]

Respect for authority is critical in all areas of life, but it runs counter to our culture's pattern. Schools struggle with student disrespect. Marital problems intensify when selfishness takes over. Job turnovers escalate where no loyalty to the employer exists. Anarchy reigns where autonomy is supreme. But God intends for us to experience inner peace rather than chaos.

If a football team can be led to victory when they follow their coach's cues, then we as Christians need to "listen up" because we have the greatest Coach of all. Submission to Christ will yield harmony, blessing, and direction for our lives.

1. Define *submission*.

2. What does a coach do for a team?

3. How does Christ do similar things for us?

4. Ephesians 1:22, 4:15, and 5:23 name Christ as the "Head" over everything, especially over us who believe in Him. What does it mean to call Christ the "Head"?

5. Jerry Kramer, a player on Vince Lombardi's football squad, said, "I had hated him at times during training camp . . . but I knew how much he had done for us and I knew how much he cared about us."[5] Just being the coach doesn't necessarily mean that the players will respond. Allegiance is earned. And Christ doesn't demand authority over us. He's earned it by who He is and what He's done. Read Philippians 2:5-11 and record reasons why Jesus is worthy to be called Lord.

Acknowledging Christ's headship intellectually is the first step to submitting to His Lordship volitionally. J. Oswald Sanders tells us,

> A clear and definite activity of the will is involved in recognizing His lordship, since He is to be Lord of all. By her "I will" the bride at the marriage altar, ideally, forever enthrones her groom in her affections. . . . A similar enthronement of Christ can result from a similar act of the will, for the same decision as enthrones Christ automatically dethrones self.[6]

6. If you have asked Christ to be the Lord of your life, summarize your experience below. Maybe you are not ready to take this step; feel free to list any reasons for your present hesitation.

7. Like sheep, our tendency is to go our own way (Isaiah 53:6). Even as Christians, we constantly struggle with selfishness. What do you do when Christ your Coach says one thing, but your self-interest tells you something else? Describe a situation when this happened to you.

8. Coach Osborne said, "When a player feels he's understood, that the coach believes in him, he'll work hard."[7] How is this true of you in your relationship with Christ your Coach?

APPLICATION

What truth from this study will help you better listen to your Coach this week?

OPTIONAL ASSIGNMENT

Use the space below to complete a Verse Analysis Bible Study of the key verse for this session. Detailed instructions on how to do this study are found in the appendix.

Hebrews 12:2

A. Read the **context before** and summarize it (Hebrews 12:1).

B. Read the **context after** and summarize it (Hebrews 12:3-11).

C. **Paraphrase** the verse.

D. Write out **questions** or problems you may have from this passage.

1.

2.

3.

4.

E. Look up and comment on **cross references** that give you further insight on this passage.

1.

2.

3.

4.

F. What **application** would you like to make from this study?

Keep the Rules

OBEDIENCE

*Similarly, if anyone competes as an athlete,
he does not receive the victor's crown unless
he competes according to the rules.*
2 Timothy 2:5

There are reasons for rules. They provide a sense of order and protect athletes from harm. Football penalties or basketball fouls are consequences players face when they disregard regulations. Those who make unethical choices because winning is all that matters to them may have to pay a high price. Such was the case for Ben Johnson during the 1988 Olympics. He experienced the glory of crossing the finish line first in the 100 meters. But 2 Timothy 2:5 was prophetic for him because he lost his victor's crown. He broke a rule by using steroids and felt the humiliation of disqualification. He was stripped of both his coveted gold medal and his reputation.[1]

God has given us commands and decrees for our own good.[2] Obedience displays our love and allegiance to Him and unlocks His bountiful blessings. If we disregard biblical guidelines and make up our own rules for life, like Ben Johnson we will reap negative consequences. Fortunately, if we're willing to acknowledge our disobedience, Christ will represent us before the Rulemaker. Not only will He wipe our record clean, but He'll even give us the power we need to obey!

1. Define *obedience*.

2. Name an athletic event you are familiar with and list a few rules connected with it.

3. What happens in this sport if someone doesn't follow the regulations?

4. What penalties affect humans when we don't follow God's guidelines?

5. What hope do we have when we break His rules (1 John 1:9)?

6. Share a time when you obeyed and felt God's blessing.

7. Obedience may not always give us pleasant results. The apostles obeyed and were brutally tortured and executed. Obedience can cost us money, status, approval, a job, or a valued relationship. Has obeying God ever cost you anything? Explain.

8. The verses listed below focus on three of the many benefits that result from our obedience. What might each of these benefits look like for you? How does this motivate you to obey God? Look up the passages and fill in the chart.

PASSAGE/BENEFIT	MOTIVATES ME BECAUSE . . .
Deuteronomy 12:28 Things will go well with you and with your children	
Joshua 1:8 Prosperity Success	
John 14:21 Loved by God Christ will reveal Himself	

9. If obedience costs you something, why should you obey?

10. The Pharisees kept all the rules but never made any points with Jesus. What did Christ identify as part of their problem (Luke 11:39-42)?

11. How can you avoid falling into the Pharisees' problem?

APPLICATION

Is there a specific area of your life in which you feel God is prompting you to be more obedient? If so, what do you think God wants you to do? What are the potential costs of doing that? What are the benefits?

OPTIONAL ASSIGNMENT

Use the space below to complete a Verse Analysis Bible Study of the key verse for this session. Detailed instructions on how to do this study are found in the appendix.

2 Timothy 2:5
A. Read the **context before** and summarize it (2 Timothy 2:1-4).

B. Read the **context after** and summarize it (2 Timothy 2:6-10).

C. **Paraphrase** the verse.

D. Write out **questions** or problems you may have from this passage.

1.

2.

3.

4.

E. Look up and comment on **cross references** that give you further insight on this passage.

1.

2.

3.

4.

F. What **application** would you like to make from this study?

Work Out a Game Plan

SETTING GOALS

*But one thing I do: Forgetting what is behind and straining
toward what is ahead, I press on toward the goal to win the
prize for which God has called me heavenward in Christ Jesus.*
Philippians 3:13-14

Jeff Blatnick's high school dream was to be part of the U.S.
Olympic wrestling team. He decided to major in physical education, train hard, and wrestle at the college level. His efforts paid
off when he was picked for the 1980 Olympic squad. Even though
disappointment set in when President Carter boycotted those
Moscow games, Jeff wasn't sidetracked from his pursuit. Another
hurdle surfaced two years later when doctors diagnosed him with
Hodgkin's Disease, requiring surgery and radiation treatments. Yet
his determination earned him a spot on the 1984 team that traveled to Los Angeles. His long-range vision and short-term goals
carried his dream to reality when he became the first American to
take home a wrestling gold medal![1]

It's no different for us. If we aim at nothing, we'll probably hit
it! Purposeful goals give us meaningful direction. In 1647 a group
of church leaders wrote the Westminster Confession to steer their
communities. Part of it states, "Man's chief end is to glorify God
and to enjoy Him forever."[2]

Praying through and writing down life objectives can free us
from involvement in tasks that God never intended for us to pur-

sue—activities that leave us exhausted and empty. Not only will life goals based on eternal values affirm our sense of purpose, but they'll also renew our perspective and carry us through the tough times. If it can work for athletes like Blatnick, it can make a difference for us as Christians too.

1. What is a goal?

2. Someone once said, "Five percent of people today make things happen, 5 percent watch things happen, and 90 percent don't know what's happening."[3] What comments do you have about this statement? If you find it helpful, in what percentile would you categorize yourself?

God is a purposeful God. The entire Bible is the story of God working out a plan step by step. His plan to rescue humans from the consequences of their foolishness has taken centuries to unfold, but God has never taken His focus off His goal.

Likewise, Christ's days were filled with purposeful activities. His consistent goal was to do His Father's will (John 6:38). Having a clear goal helped Him make on-the-spot decisions.

3. What did Christ tell the people in Capernaum when they asked Him to stay and continue ministering to them (Luke 4:43)? How do His words reflect a focused goal?

4. What was Paul's goal in life before his encounter with Christ (Acts 26:9-11)?

5. The direction of Paul's life changed radically. What new path did Jesus ask him to pursue in Acts 26:12-18?

6. Paul said he wanted to win the prize for which God had called him heavenward (Philippians 3:14). His passion to know Christ energized his life. Rewrite Philippians 3:8 in your own words.

7. What does Philippians 3:8 say about the level of Paul's passion for His goal?

8. Just as Paul's goals shifted when he met Christ, so should ours. What "game plan" does Jesus have in mind for us believers (2 Corinthians 5:15)?

9. Many people find it helpful to pray about life goals and write them out. How does Ephesians 5:15-17 support this idea?

10. What guidelines does James 4:13-17 give us when we are making plans? Circle three.
   • We should never make plans.
   • Trying to make money is sinful.
   • Having a sane perspective on our mortality is healthy.
   • Our pursuits should be surrendered to God's will.
   • Self-centered boasting is appropriate when we've done a good job.
   • Awareness of God's will without obedience is sin.

APPLICATION

Using the following suggestions, write your own life goals on a separate sheet of paper.

1. What Bible verses have been significant to you in your life? Write two to four passages. It's good to have at least one focusing on your relationship to God and one that could direct you to a ministry for Him.

2. With these verses in mind, write goals that reflect what you want to do with your life regarding your relationship to God and to others. Make them broad enough for all of life's circumstances. (For example: *Proverbs 3:5-6.* I want to get to know God better so I can trust Him more and look to Him for direction in my life, rather than try to figure out things in my own understanding. *Romans 1:16.* I want to move into my relationships with both Christians and unbelievers in a way that demonstrates that I believe the gospel is the power of God and am not ashamed of Christ.

OPTIONAL ASSIGNMENT

Use the space on the following page to complete a Verse Analysis Bible Study of the key verses for this session. Detailed instructions on how to do this study are found in the appendix.

Philippians 3:13-14

A. Read the **context before** and summarize it (Philippians 3:7-12).

B. Read the **context after** and summarize it (Philippians 3:15-21).

C. **Paraphrase** the passage.

D. Write out **questions** or problems you may have from this passage.
   1.

   2.

   3.

   4.

E. Look up and comment on **cross references** that give you further insight on this passage.
   1.

   2.

   3.

   4.

F. What **application** would you like to make from this study?

Get into Shape

DISCIPLINES OF THE CHRISTIAN LIFE

*Have nothing to do with godless myths and old wives' tales;
rather, train yourself to be godly. For physical training
is of some value, but godliness has value for all things,
holding promise for both the present life
and the life to come.*
1 Timothy 4:7-8

Athletes train hard to get into shape and to keep their game sharp, knowing that no pain means no gain. A few years ago a native Californian named Lindsay Davenport attained her dream . . . she accepted the 1996 Olympic tennis gold medal while "The Star Spangled Banner" paid tribute to America. But the path to victory wasn't easy. After barely making the U.S. team, she went into strict training. She lost twenty pounds and worked day after long day with her coach.[1]

Discipline is critical for athletic success and foundational for our spiritual lives as well. The apostle Paul reminds us in 1 Timothy 4:7-8 that there is great value in training ourselves to be godly. Although it takes effort, discipline should not be viewed as drudgery! Richard Foster says, "God intends the disciplines of the spiritual life to be for ordinary human beings, best exercised in the midst of our normal daily activities. They are not some dull drudgery aimed at exterminating laughter from the face of the earth. Joy is the keynote of all the disciplines."[2]

Like Lindsay, we have a choice: to train or not to train. We won't develop our spiritual muscles unless we consistently work out in God's gymnasium using His disciplines of grace.

1. Define *discipline*.

2. Name a sport and tell what kind of training is needed to prepare for it.

If you're in sports, you know what discipline is. Regular practices, hours at the gym after work, a strict diet, a tight schedule, shin splints, cramps, and other strains and sprains. This is the life of an athlete. But an athlete's tough regimen isn't the only kind of discipline that's important.[3]

3. The spiritual disciplines are meant to help us grow as Christians. For the ones listed below and on page 35, name one benefit gained from the discipline.

DISCIPLINE	BENEFIT
Meditation on Bible Joshua 1:8	
Corporate worship 2 Chronicles 29:28-30	

DISCIPLINE	BENEFIT
Silence and stillness Psalm 46:10	
Fasting Acts 13:2-3	
Prayer Philippians 4:6-7	

Living a disciplined life is not always the same as living a godly life. It is possible to pray, fast, give, memorize, and meditate on the Word without moving closer to God. Three traps to avoid are:

- Using a spiritual discipline as an end in itself rather than as a means to the end of knowing Christ in a deeper way.
- Feeling prideful about your disciplined life: "I'm such a good Christian because I do all these things in order to know God."
- Putting great effort into spiritual disciplines and little effort into "justice, mercy, and faithfulness" (Matthew 23:23).

4. Which is a greater temptation for you: to practice spiritual disciplines diligently but fall into one of the above three traps, or to be lazy about spiritual disciplines?

5. Write your comments after reading the following quotes:

In contemporary society our Adversary majors in three things: noise, hurry, and crowds. If he can keep us engaged in "much-ness" and manyness: he will rest satisfied.[4]

Muse was the name given to an ancient Greek god who spent much time in solitude and thinking. The statue of "The Thinker" is the artistic concept of deep concentration. Add an "a" to the beginning of muse and you have amuse . . . sports, games, television, and a score of other tools used by the enemy.[5]

To be in the presence of God is to change. That is why meditation is so threatening. It boldly calls us to enter into the living presence of God.[6]

In silence and quietness of heart a devout soul profits much and learns the hidden meaning of Scripture, and finds many sweet tears of devotion as well.[7]

APPLICATION

Set aside an hour this week for solitude and silence. Find some way to get away from noise and other people. During this time you can take a gentle walk, read a little Scripture and think about it, pray a bit, or just let your mind relax. No reading other than the Bible, and no entertainment! What kind of noise goes through your mind when you are alone and still? Can you tolerate the silence long enough to hear God? Ask God what regular discipline He would like you to practice each week.

Celebration of Discipline by Richard Foster is an excellent resource for you if you'd like to develop more in this area.

OPTIONAL ASSIGNMENT

Use the space below to complete a Verse Analysis Bible Study of the key verses for this session. Detailed instructions on how to do this study are found in the appendix.

1 Timothy 4:7-8

A. Read the **context before** and summarize it (1 Timothy 4:1-6).

B. Read the **context after** and summarize it (1 Timothy 4:9-10).

C. **Paraphrase** the verses.

D. Write out **questions** or problems you may have from this passage.
   1.

   2.

   3.

   4.

E. Look up and comment on **cross references** that give you further insight on this passage.

1.

2.

3.

4.

F. What **application** would you like to make from this study?

Work as a Team

RELATING IN THE BODY OF CHRIST

Do not think of yourself more highly than you ought. . . .
Just as each of us has one body with many members,
and these members do not all have the same function,
so in Christ we who are many form one body,
and each member belongs to all the others.
Romans 12:3-5

A team that works together is hard to beat! When the Chicago Bulls played the Phoenix Suns for the 1993 basketball championship, Chicago trailed by two points with only thirteen seconds of play left. Michael Jordan passed the ball in bounds to Armstrong, received it back, and dribbled down the court. But instead of shooting as everyone expected, he shoveled the ball to Scottie Pippen, who bounced it to Horace Grant, who quickly put it in the hands of their open player just beyond the three-point line. John Paxton connected! The amazing team effort of all five men earned the Bulls a trophy.[1]

What does it feel like to be part of a team? Football player Jeff Makovicka, said this: "The neat thing about sports is that it brings people together from different walks of life. You become brothers with your teammates regardless of their backgrounds, and that is really a positive experience."[2] Another player, Tyrone Williams, said, "When you get 15 players unified, striving for one goal, it can be pretty powerful."[3]

So it is with Christians. Men and women from different walks of life bond quickly as brothers and sisters because of Jesus. We are more than a team—we are intricately tied to one another like body parts. We don't all have the same function, but we belong together in Christ. God chose to use us as His body to accomplish great feats. When all the parts are unified, striving for one goal under Christ's headship, it is incredibly powerful!

1. Define *synergy*.

2. Explain how synergy operates in both an athletic team and the body of Christ.

3. Read how the early church functioned as a team in Acts 4:32-33. What was their attitude toward each other and toward their possessions? What resulted from their unity?

4. What other benefits can we experience when we relate closely to others?

   Proverbs 27:17

   Ecclesiastes 4:9-10

5. Former Dodgers manager Tommy Lasorda said, "My responsibility is to get my 25 guys playing for the name on the front of their uniforms, not the one on their back."[4] "Hot dogging" is frowned on in sports. Neither is there room for it in the Christian life. Explain why by using Romans 12:3-5 and 1 Corinthians 12:12-25.

6. Just as the morale on a basketball team can be fired up or deflated by the interaction of its members, so we as Christians affect others in the body of Christ. Fill in the chart below that outlines actions we can take to encourage other believers.

PASSAGE/ POSITIVE ACTION	HOW I COULD DEMONSTRATE IT THIS WEEK
Luke 6:31 Do for others what I'd want them to do for me	
Philippians 2:4 Be more concerned about others than myself	
Ephesians 4:29 Speak what will build others up	
1 Peter 3:8-9 Sympathize with others Live in harmony with them Be humble	

7. Every person in the body of Christ is important. We all have different gifts, and no one is insignificant, no matter how minor a role he or she plays. The Bible lists spiritual gifts in Romans 12:6-8 and 1 Corinthians 12:8-10. What gift or gifts do you feel you might have?

If you don't know what your gifts are, here are some steps you could take toward finding out:

- Take a spiritual gifts test. Your church may use one or know of one.
- Buy a book on spiritual gifts. Many of them contain self-tests.
- For many people, the best way to discover their gifts is to start doing something to serve others. Volunteer at your church or another ministry. Each time you try something, you'll learn more about what fits you and what doesn't.

8. Besides spiritual gifts, we each have different skills and talents. What are some of the abilities you feel you possess?

9. How can God use these on His team?

APPLICATION
How can you participate on God's team this week? How can you share with others in getting something done that God wants done?

OPTIONAL ASSIGNMENT
Use the space below to complete a Verse Analysis Bible Study of the key verses for this session. Detailed instructions on how to do this study are found in the appendix.

Romans 12:3-5
A. Read the **context before** and summarize it (Romans 12:1-2).

B. Read the **context after** and summarize it (Romans 12:6-8).

C. **Paraphrase** the passage.

D. Write out **questions** or problems you may have from this passage.
   1.

   2.

   3.

   4.

E. Look up and comment on **cross references** that give you further insight on this passage.

1.

2.

3.

4.

F. What **application** would you like to make from this study?

Be a Good Sport

CHARACTER UNDER PRESSURE

But you, man of God, flee from all of this, and pursue
righteousness, godliness, faith, love, endurance and gentleness.
Fight the good fight of the faith. Take hold of the eternal life
to which you were called when you made your good
confession in the presence of many witnesses.
1 Timothy 6:11-12

Maybe the umpire has just made a bad call or an opponent has ticked you off. Or maybe the morale on the whole team is rotten because of a seven-game losing streak. Maybe you brush off disappointments and say, "That's the way the old ball bounces." But that's not easy to do. Athletes are often faced with a question: "How can we be good sports whether we're winning or losing?" Whether we're playing a set in tennis or are involved in a game of chess, how do we get beyond a competitive spirit so that we can enjoy the striving just as much as the arriving?

Not many people have heard of a German named Luz Long. He competed against Jesse Owens in the long jump at the 1936 Berlin Olympics. After Jesse fouled on his first attempt, he said that Luz gave him a friendly tip that helped Jesse qualify on his next jump. Jesse won the gold medal and Luz took home the silver.[1] But Luz Long's unselfish act cemented a lifelong friendship in this world and captured the approval of another Friend in the heavens.

God is in the process of chiseling out our character through our circumstances. Even if life doesn't seem fair, the way we respond matters! Just as an athlete represents his or her school, city, state, or nation, we as Christians are God's ambassadors. Our words, actions, and reactions reflect on Him:

> *You are writing a gospel, a chapter each day,*
> *By the deeds that you do and words that you say.*
> *Men read what you write . . . distorted or true;*
> *What is the gospel according to you?*[2]

1. Define *character*.

Success in sports is often measured by winning. An old saying tells us, "It doesn't matter whether you win or lose, but how you play the game." But Vince Lombardi said, "If winning isn't so important, why do we keep score?"[3]

2. What is potentially good about a competitive spirit?

3. What problems can arise because of an unhealthy competitive attitude?

4. How is success in the Christian life measured? Paul challenges us to "run in such a way that you may win" (1 Corinthians 9:24, NASB). What do you think he means by this? How does God measure success or winning?

46

Competitive events for the athlete and circumstances in life for the believer set the stage where two character qualities (or the lack of them) are exhibited: self-esteem and self-control.

Self-Esteem

Chris Evert said, "Tennis has been my world since I was six. It defined who I was. I had a high esteem for myself following victory, the opposite after a loss."[4] Yet our sense of identity should not be wrapped up in our performance, but in the image reflected to us by God.

5. What do the following verses say about your worth from God's point of view?

Jeremiah 31:3

Zephaniah 3:17

6. When our identity is wrapped up in our appearance, abilities, or status, we become vulnerable to either end of a negative pendulum: pride or depression. In areas of our strengths, what does God tell us in Jeremiah 9:23 about boasting?

7. In areas of our weaknesses, what does Christ promise in 2 Corinthians 12:9?

8. A good athlete exhibits self-control. This quality is equally important in all our relationships. Anger often results when something blocks our goals. How does James 4:1-2 describe the roots of anger?

9. From the verses below, summarize what the Bible teaches about anger and what can be done to control it.

PASSAGE	WHAT WE LEARN ABOUT ANGER	WHAT CAN HELP US CONROL IT
Proverbs 12:16		
James 1:19-20		

If you have trouble controlling your anger, Philippians 4:13 promises that God will give you the strength to do so if you actively pursue His help.

APPLICATION
In which area, self-esteem or self-control, would you like to move closer to God's ideal? What steps can you take? What help from God do you need to ask for?

OPTIONAL ASSIGNMENT
Use the space below to complete a Verse Analysis Bible Study of the key verses for this session. Detailed instructions on how to do this study are found in the appendix.

1 Timothy 6:11-12
A. Read the **context before** and summarize it (1 Timothy 6:3-10).

B. Read the **context after** and summarize it (1 Timothy 6:13-16).

C. **Paraphrase** the passage.

D. Write out **questions** or problems you may have from this passage.
    1.

    2.

    3.

    4.

E. Look up and comment on **cross references** that give you further insight on this passage.
    1.

    2.

    3.

    4.

F. What **application** would you like to make from this study?

Take a Time Out

REGROUPING WITH GOD

Even youths grow tired and weary,
and young men stumble and fall;
but those who hope in the LORD will renew their strength.
They will soar on wings like eagles;
they will run and not grow weary,
they will walk and not be faint.
Isaiah 40:30-31

When the whistle blows for a time out, athletes draw aside from the intensity of the game to get new direction and encouragement. Coaches give pep talks before the action starts, during the half-time, and sometimes after the game. Vince Lombardi, a former head coach of the Green Bay Packers, won five NFL titles and two Super Bowls. His team paid attention to what he said because he instilled in them an incentive to win. Once after a tough loss, he gathered them around him and emphasized their need to refocus on the fundamentals. "OK, we go back to the basics." He held the ball high for all to see and continued, "Gentlemen, this is a football."[1]

It's just as important for us as Christians to detach from the busyness of the world—to get back to the basics and gain fresh perspective from God about our lives. Christ modeled this by drawing aside to linger prayerfully with His Father. Charles Hummel said, "Prayerful waiting on God is indispensable to effective service. Like the time out in a football game, it enables us to catch our breath and fix new strategy."[2] Neglecting to seek God's help is a subtle form of arrogant autonomy. Hanging out with God is our way of saying, "Lord, I love You. I need Your direction today."

1. What is a time out?

2. How can an athlete benefit from a time out?

3. From the passages below, note what Moses and Nehemiah did during their time out, and write what happened directly after their seclusion with God.

PASSAGE	WHAT THEY DID	WHAT HAPPENED
Moses Exodus 34:1-8, 27-29		
Nehemiah Nehemiah 1:1–2:6		

4. List the benefits of drawing aside with God and tell why this is important for us in society today.

PASSAGE	BENEFIT	WHY IT IS IMPORTANT TODAY
Psalm 32:8		
Isaiah 55:1-3		
Matthew 11:28-30		
James 1:5		

Even when we're aware of the benefits, we often don't get the time with God we need. Jesus knows our struggles and has worked through every possible reason that would hinder us. See how He handled each situation below.

Reason #1: "I'm too busy"

No one had more to do than Christ, yet He made time to get with God. A. E. Whiteham wrote, "Here in this Man is adequate purpose . . . inward rest, that gives an air of leisure to His crowded life."[3]

5. After teaching all day and feeding five thousand people, what did Jesus do (Mark 6:45-56)?

Reason #2: "I won't be able to finish my work."

Near the end of His life, Christ was able to say that He had completed His work. Charles Hummel wrote, "Jesus' prayerful waiting for God's instructions freed Him from the tyranny of the urgent. It gave Him a sense of direction, set a steady pace, and enabled Him to do every task God assigned."[4] After getting time with God, Christ opted out of tasks others thought He should do.

6. How did Jesus make time for God in Mark 1:35-38?

Reason #3: "I'm afraid! God might ask me to do something too hard to do."

Jesus had similar feelings but knew that avoiding God wouldn't solve anything. Fear is a strong factor in sinful choices we make. Larry Crabb wrote, "Only the intrusion of a person who can relieve our terror by providing us with both a guarantee of a perfect relationship and a taste of it now is a strong enough influence to help us shift directions."[5]

7. Jesus knew in the Garden of Gethsemane that God was His only hope. How did He deal with fear (Luke 22:41-42)?

Reason #4: "I'm smart enough to handle life without running to God for everything."

Wrong! If Christ found it necessary to depend on God, are we any less needful? P. T. Forsyth said, "The root of all sin is self-sufficiency—independence from God. When we fail to wait prayerfully for God's guidance and strength we are saying with our actions, if not our lips, that we do not need him."[6] That is ultimate arrogance! Christ got time with God before making major decisions.

8. What major decision did Christ make in Luke 6:12-16, and how did He prepare for it?

9. What distracts you from taking regular time outs? Are any of the above reasons relevant to you?

APPLICATION

What would it take for you to get a four-hour stretch of time (or more) alone with God in the next couple of months?

OPTIONAL ASSIGNMENT

Use the space below to complete a Verse Analysis Bible Study of the key verses for this session. Detailed instructions on how to do this study are found in the appendix.

Isaiah 40:30-31

A. Read the **context before** and summarize it (Isaiah 40:27-29).

B. Read the **context after** and summarize it (Isaiah 41:1-10).

C. **Paraphrase** the passage.

D. Write out **questions** or problems you may have from this passage.
   1.

   2.

   3.

   4.

E. Look up and comment on **cross references** that give you further insight on this passage.
   1.

   2.

   3.

   4.

F. What **application** would you like to make from this study?

Scout Your Opponent

KNOWING YOUR ENEMY

You were running a good race. Who cut in on you and kept you from obeying the truth? That kind of persuasion does not come from the one who calls you.
Galatians 5:7-8

Mike Hebert didn't build winning teams and become NCAA coach of the year without strategies. He didn't just take the University of Illinois women's volleyball team from the cellar to the Big Ten championship—he also was selected to coach the USA team that traveled to the Pan American Games in 1991. His success has come from his determination to understand everything he can about his team's opponents. Mike believes it's important to know who has the highest hitting percentages, gets the most sets, and passes and serves well. He also finds out which of his competitor's players are the stabilizers of the team and which ones handle pressure poorly. He feels it's equally important to understand the strengths, weaknesses, and tendencies of the opposing coach. All this insight helps him train his teams to go into games better prepared with tactics that work.[1]

Christians aren't playing a game. We have a real adversary who is doing everything he can to destroy us! Coaches use scouts to give them reports about the strengths and weaknesses of the other team. We have a manual already written up that helps us understand our opponent's basic schemes. God's Word gives us insights into both our opponent and ourselves. It also outlines both offensive and defensive strategies that will overthrow our Adversary. We need to study our manual well because following its guidelines may make the difference between victory and defeat!

1. Define *victory*.

2. Read John 8:44 and 1 Peter 5:8. Who is our major enemy and how is he described?

3. What are his strategies against believers (2 Corinthians 11:3)?

4. What are his strategies against unbelievers (2 Corinthians 4:4)?

5. Have you had any experience with the things you described the enemy doing in questions 2 through 4? If so, what have been one or two of your experiences?

6. The Bible suggests equipment we can use to defend against such schemes. What are some of our resources listed in Ephesians 6:13-18?

7. The "world" is another opposition that threatens us. According to the *Expository Dictionary of Bible Words*, "As a theological term *kosmos* (world) portrays human society as a system warped by sin . . . a dark system operating on basic principles that are not of God."[2] The "world" includes political systems, economic forces, social problems, media empires, ungodly things that "everybody" believes—all those big things that dominate much of life on earth. What is one aspect of the "world" that particularly hinders you from living a fruitful Christian life?

8. What can give us victory over the "world" (John 17:14-18)?

9. How could that source of victory help you in your struggle with the "world"?

Another foe that we battle is our own flesh. In the New Testament, the word *flesh* is not equivalent to your physical body. Your body is fundamentally good because God created it, but *flesh* "emphasizes humanity's moral inadequacy . . . energized by evil desires and guided by perceptions that distort God's will and His nature."[3] Fleshly enemies include things that are not strictly physical, such as sexual promiscuity, a temper, hatred, jealousy, selfish ambition, and envy (Galatians 5:19-21). Addictions fall into this category too.

10. What is one fleshly enemy that is a problem for you?

11. How can you hope to overcome the pull within you toward fleshly cravings and reactions? Romans 8:12-17 says you should "put to death" the misdeeds of the flesh by the power of the "Spirit of God." What does that mean? How can you access the Spirit's power to put to death your fleshly enemy? (Note: This may be a process of repeatedly putting something to death, rather than a quick-and-easy job.)

Ultimately, our victory is assured. God gives us the victory through the work of Christ (1 Corinthians 15:57). But until we leave this earth, we will have continual skirmishes with our three enemies: the devil, the world, and the flesh.

APPLICATION

In the world of sports, scouting the opponent helps a team better prepare both offensively and defensively. From the truths in this session, what is one thing you can include in your spiritual "game strategy" either offensively or defensively to ensure victory this week?

OPTIONAL ASSIGNMENT

Use the space on the following page to complete a Verse Analysis Bible Study of the key verses for this session. Detailed instructions on how to do this study are found in the appendix.

Galatians 5:7-8

A. Read the **context before** and summarize it (Galatians 5:1-6).

B. Read the **context after** and summarize it (Galatians 5:9-10).

C. **Paraphrase** the passage.

D. Write out **questions** or problems you may have from this passage.
   1.

   2.

   3.

   4.

E. Look up and comment on **cross references** that give you further insight on this passage.
   1.

   2.

   3.

   4.

F. What **application** would you like to make from this study?

11

Hang in There

PERSEVERING IN ADVERSITY

*However, I consider my life worth nothing to me, if only I may
finish the race and complete the task the Lord Jesus has given
me—the task of testifying to the gospel of God's grace.*
Acts 20:24

It's not uncommon for athletes to struggle with injury setbacks,
emotional slumps, or physical exhaustion. It takes tenacity to
press ahead. Dan Marino, a former Miami Dolphins quarterback,
expressed it this way: "I think it just comes down to being men-
tally tough. If things don't go well for you, you've got to keep
going—keep throwing the ball."[1]

At the age of seventeen, Michael Chang faced formidable odds
before making it to the finals of the tennis French Open in 1989. Leg
cramps plagued him during the fourth round. The semifinal was a
marathon of play lasting four hours and five minutes. Chang won,
but he suffered heat exhaustion and had to be carried to the locker
room. Prospects for victory didn't look promising during the finals
when he fell behind two sets to one. But his perseverance paid off:
he became the youngest Grand Slam winner in tennis history.[2]

A good athlete doesn't throw in the towel when his or her stam-
ina is stretched to the limit. And as Christians we need strength
when we face our own endurance contests—chronic illness, financial
blows, family problems, school pressures, job insecurities, or ministry
frustration. These can sap our emotional and spiritual vitality.

Sometimes it takes courage just to hang in there when we feel overwhelmed, knowing that persevering through adversity builds our character and yields both earthly and eternal rewards.

1. Define *perseverance*.

2. Just as a good athlete displays confidence without cockiness, healthy perseverance is not something we gut out with fleshly pride. What do you think it looks like in practice to "do everything through him who gives me strength" (Philippians 4:13)?

3. A professional golfer named Gary Player said, "Great athletes have an inner strength, something you can't define."[3] Give an example of an athlete or a Christian who has displayed this.

4. Former college quarterback Turner Gil said, "Adversity has a way of calling forth those qualities in us that are most enduring and important."[4] What qualities do trials develop in a Christian (Romans 5:3-5)?

5. Do you think trials do this automatically for all Christians, or do we have to cooperate in some way?

6. Think of a trial you've observed a friend or family member face. Did that hardship build perseverance, character, and hope in his or her life? If so, in what ways? If not, why do you suppose that didn't happen?

7. We often think of adversity as some sort of crisis. But facing mundane routines and dealing with subtle circumstances like unanswered prayers, disappointments, or fatigue call for as much perseverance as dealing with major disasters. Think of something mundane in your life, and describe how it requires perseverance.

8. Losing games or dealing with injuries is tough. An athlete has to face his or her own weaknesses. How do you typically deal with weakness?

9. Christ says His power is made perfect in our weakness (2 Corinthians 12:9-10). Have you ever experienced that? What was that like, or what do you imagine it could be like?

10. Complete this chart, which outlines factors that can encourage us during hard times.

PASSAGE	WHAT GOD PROMISES	WHY THIS IS IMPORTANT
Psalm 34:18		
Romans 8:35-39		

11. What are some of the difficult issues you are facing or have faced over the past few months?

12. In New Testament times it was customary to crown a victorious athlete with laurel leaves. What is promised in James 1:12 to those who persevere? What do you think "the crown of life" means?

APPLICATION

What has most encouraged or challenged you from this study?
How is it personally relevant to you?

OPTIONAL ASSIGNMENT

Use the space below to complete a Verse Analysis Bible Study of
the key verse for this session. Detailed instructions on how to do
this study are found in the appendix.

Acts 20:24
A. Read the **context before** and summarize it (Acts 20:22-23).

B. Read the **context after** and summarize it (Acts 20:25-32).

C. **Paraphrase** the verse.

D. Write out **questions** or problems you may have from this
   passage.
   1.

   2.

   3.

   4.

E. Look up and comment on **cross references** that give you further insight on this passage.
    1.

    2.

    3.

    4.

F. What **application** would you like to make from this study?

Go for the Gold

FINISHING WELL

*I have fought the good fight, I have finished the race,
I have kept the faith. Now there is in store for me
the crown of righteousness.*
2 Timothy 4:7-8

Derek Redmond was the British 400-meter runner favored to win the 1992 Olympics in Barcelona. But fifty meters from sure victory, he collapsed in pain with a torn hamstring in his right leg. After the other runners finished their race, all eyes turned to Derek, who was struggling to rise. They watched as Derek's father hastened from the stands to his side. He provided Derek with a shoulder to lean on as the young man hobbled toward the finish line.[1]

Starting a marathon is simple. Completing it is another story. We as Christians may find ourselves struggling to finish well. In our weariness, we're tempted to quit or to live half-heartedly. But God encourages us to keep on the path, even when it's hard. Ted Frederick, author of *Running the Race,* wrote, "For the spiritual athlete to endure means to keep his gaze toward Jesus Christ who stands at the finish line of life. The pain and discomfort fades in the pleasure of doing His will."[2]

Focused on His Father, Jesus finished His work on earth. Paul leaned on Christ and was able to finish well, confidently looking forward to his reward. At the end of Derek Redmond's race, his father lifted him up and enabled him to finish well. With his dad at his side, not even an injury could force him to give up. We too have a heavenly Father at our side who will hold us up whether we run or limp across the finish line. He's eager to present us with the prize He has prepared for us.

1. David Lloyd George said, "There's nothing so fatal to character as half finished tasks."[3] What does it mean to finish something well?

2. The Olympic Creed reads, "The most important thing in the Olympic Games is not to win but to take part, just as the most important thing in life is not the triumph but the struggle. The essential thing is not to have conquered but to have fought well."[4] How did Derek Redmond illustrate this?

3. Eric Liddle, the gold medalist whose life was portrayed in the movie *Chariots of Fire,* expressed the reward he felt as he raced: "God made me fast. When I run, I feel his pleasure. To win is to honor him."[5] Explain what you think he meant by that comment.

Winning has more to do with honoring God by being faithful (Matthew 25:21) than it does with striving to win a trophy for selfish gain. The apostle Paul's concern was not for individual fame but to please Jesus. He wanted to press on toward the goal to win the prize for which God had called him heavenward (Philippians 3:14).

4. Give a hypothetical example of a Christian who appears to be a winner, but in God's eyes is actually a loser?

5. Give a hypothetical example of a Christian who appears to be a loser, but in God's eyes is actually a winner?

God rewards the Christian who goes for the gold. The New Testament writers speak over and over about victory crowns: "the crown of righteousness" (2 Timothy 4:7-8), "the crown of glory" (1 Peter 5:4), and "the crown of life" (Revelation 2:10).

6. Have you ever won a prize? How did it make you feel?

7. Just as God finished His work of creation (Genesis 2:2) and Jesus finished the work His Father gave Him (John 4:34), Paul longed to finish well. Write out Acts 20:24 in your own words.

8. What factors could cause you to feel like giving up and not finish well?

9. Sometimes we feel overwhelmed with life. When a visitor, amazed by the daily tasks Mother Teresa faced in her Calcutta mission, asked her how she hoped to feed all the hungry

people that came to her, Mother Teresa replied, "One mouth at a time."[6] How can this be an encouragement to us?

APPLICATION
Derek Redmond relied on his dad to cross the finish line. Talk to your Father about your concerns in running this Christian marathon. Ask for His help to finish well!

OPTIONAL ASSIGNMENT
Use the space below to complete a Verse Analysis Bible Study of the key verses for this session. Detailed instructions on how to do this study are found in the appendix.

2 Timothy 4:7-8
A. Read the **context before** and summarize it (2 Timothy 4:1-6).

B. Read the **context after** and summarize it (2 Timothy 4:9-18).

C. **Paraphrase** the passage.

D. Write out **questions** or problems you may have from this passage.
    1.

    2.

    3.

    4.

E. Look up and comment on **cross references** that give you further insight on this passage.
    1.

    2.

    3.

    4.

F. What **application** would you like to make from this study?

How to Complete a Verse Analysis Bible Study

*T*he method below will help you dig deeper into the truths of God's Word. Whether you do these studies for your own personal benefit or as a basis for group discussion, you will enhance your understanding of each of the topics studied in this book.

A. *Context before:* Read thoughtfully through the passage in parentheses. This is the context that precedes the key verse(s). Then, in a sentence or two, summarize the major thoughts of this passage. Be thinking about how this passage relates to the Scripture you are studying.

B. *Context after:* Again, read thoughtfully through the passage in parentheses. This is the context following the key verse(s). Then, in a sentence or two, summarize the major thoughts of the passage. Be thinking about how this passage relates to the Scripture you are studying.

C. *Paraphrase:* Write out the key verse(s) in your own words. This is a method of meditation that will open up new insights and help you understand the passage more clearly.

D. *Questions:* Write out questions or problems you have after reading the key verse(s) and its context. These may be real questions that you want answered or possible questions you think others might wonder about. You could think through *who, what, why, where, when,* and *how* questions. Or, you could jot down random queries that come to mind as you meditate on the passage.

E. *Cross references:* Write down the references and thoughts from additional passages that support the basic concept of the passage you are studying. Many Bibles contain cross references in the margins. Additionally, you may have a concordance in the back of your Bible, or you could buy a more thorough stand-alone concordance. Other Bible study aids—such as topical Bibles, Bible dictionaries, and commentaries—include cross references.

F. *Application:* As you look over the study you have just completed, ask God if there is anything He wants you to apply to your life. It can be something you want to:

1. *Remember*—a truth you'd like to meditate on through the week. Example: "I haven't thought much about the fact that God has marked out a unique race for me to run. I want to think about that more this week."

2. *Do*—an action you sense God is asking you to do. Example: "I'm going to use my time on free evenings this month reading a Christian historical novel rather than watching television."

3. *Use*—an action you plan to take involving another person. Example: "I will call Mary and let her know that her perseverance in her walk with God has been a big motivation for me spiritually."

Notes

Session 1

1. Bud Greenspan, ed., *Wilma: The Story of Wilma Rudolph* (New York: New American Library, 1977); quoted in Gordon Thiessen, *Cross Training Manual* (Grand Island, NE: Cross Training Publishing, 1991), p. 38.
2. Karl M. Woods, *Sports Success Book* (Austin, TX: Copperfield Press, 1985), p. 70.
3. Thiessen, p. 39.
4. Melanie Jongsma, *Fit for Life* (South Holland, IL: The Bible League, 1992), p. 26.

Session 2

1. Nolan Ryan, *Miracle Man* (Dallas: Word, 1992), p. 222.
2. "Athletes Who Are Leading by Example," *Sports Spectrum,* March/April 1991, p. 12; quoted in Gordon Thiessen, *Cross Training Manual* (Grand Island, NE: Cross Training Publishing, 1991), p. 43.
3. "Madison Square Gartner," *Sports Spectrum,* November/December 1990, p. 24; quoted in Thiessen, p. 13.

Session 3

1. Keith Zimmer, *Behind Every Champion* (Lincoln, NE: Dageforde Publishing, 1996), p. 18.
2. Zimmer, p. 69.
3. Zimmer, p. 71.
4. Tom Osborne, *More Than Winning* (Nashville, TN: Nelson, 1985), p. 51.
5. Craig Clifford, *Coaching for Character* (Champaign, IL: Human Kinetics Publishers, 1997), p. 74.
6. J. Oswald Sanders, *Pursuit of the Holy* (Grand Rapids, MI: Zondervan, 1972), p. 31.
7. Osborne, p. 51.

Session 4

1. *1997 Information Please Sports Almanac* (Boston, MA: Houghton Mifflin Company, 1997), p. 524.
2. Deuteronomy 10:13.

Session 5

1. John and Kathy Hillman, *Devotions from the World of Sports* (Colorado Springs: Chariot Victor Publishing, 1998), August 18.
2. Joel R. Beeke and Sinclair B. Ferguson, *Reformed Confessions Harmonized* (Grand Rapids, MI: Baker, 1999), p. xiii.
3. Author unknown.

Session 6

1. John and Kathy Hillman, *Devotions from the World of Sports* (Colorado Springs: Chariot Victor Publishing, 1998), August 2.
2. Richard J. Foster, *Celebration of Discipline* (San Francisco: Harper & Row, 1978), p. 1.
3. Melanie Jongsma, *Fit for Life* (South Holland, IL: The Bible League, 1992), p. 4.
4. Foster, p. 13.
5. The Navigators, *Primer on Meditation* (Colorado Springs, CO: NavPress), p. 4.
6. Foster, p. 19.
7. Thomas à Kempis, *The Imitation of Christ*, (Garden City, NY: Image Books, 1955), p. 57.

Session 7

1. John and Kathy Hillman, *Devotions from the World of Sports* (Colorado Springs: Chariot Victor Publishing, 1998), June 20.
2. Charlie Jones, *What Makes Winners Win* (Secaucus, NJ: Carol Publishing Group, 1997), p. 71.
3. Keith Zimmer, *Behind Every Champion* (Lincoln, NE: Dageforde Publishing, 1996), p. 18.
4. Jones, p. 46.

Session 8

1. Hank Nuwer, *The Legend of Jesse Owens* (New York: Grolier, 1998), p. 91.
2. The Navigators, *Growing Strong in God's Family* (Colorado Springs, CO: NavPress, 1999), p. 83.
3. Gordon Thiessen, *Cross Training Manual* (Grand Island, NE: Cross Training Publishing, 1991), p. 2.
4. Thiessen, p. 3.

Session 9

1. Gordon Thiessen, *Cross Training Manual* (Grand Island, NE: Cross Training Publishing, 1991), p. 116.
2. Charles Hummel, *Tyranny of the Urgent* (Downers Grove, IL: InterVarsity, 1967); quoted in The Navigators, *Growing Strong in God's Family* (Colorado Springs, CO: NavPress, 1999), p. 25.
3. Quoted in Hummel, p. 24.
4. Hummel, p. 25.
5. Larry Crabb, *Understanding Who You Are* (Colorado Springs, CO: NavPress, 1997), p. 23.
6. Quoted in Hummel, p. 25.

Session 10

1. Mike Hebert, *Insights and Strategies for Winning Volleyball* (Champaign, IL: Leisure Press, 1991), p. 183 and back cover.
2. Lawrence O. Richards, *Expository Dictionary of Bible Words* (Grand Rapids, MI: Zondervan, 1985), p. 639.
3. Richards, p. 285.

Session 11

1. Charlie Jones, *What Makes Winners Win* (Secaucus, NJ: Carol Publishing Group, 1997), p. 30.
2. John and Kathy Hillman, *Devotions from the World of Sports* (Colorado Springs: Chariot Victor Publishing, 1998), June 15.
3. Jones, p. 151.
4. Tom Osborne, *More Than Winning* (Nashville, TN: Nelson, 1985), p. 83.

Session 12

1. "A Weak Leg—A Strong Father," advertisement, *Lufthansa Magazin*, April 2000, p. 89.
2. Ted Frederick, *Running the Race* (Grand Rapids, MI: Baker, 1979), p. 104.
3. Frederick, p. 103.
4. *Encyclopedia Americana*, vol. 20 (Danbury, CN: Grolier, 1997), p. 716.
5. Gordon Thiessen, *Cross Training Manual* (Grand Island, NE: Cross Training Publishing, 1991), p. 14.
6. Richard G. Capen Jr., *Finish Strong* (Grand Rapids, MI: Zondervan, 1996), p. xxvi.

About the Author

Kathy Johnston and her husband, Charlie, have been on full-time staff with the Navigators since 1970. Though they've been missionaries in Vancouver, Canada, and in the Philippines, they are currently ministering in Omaha, Nebraska. They have been blessed with three children: Shelley, Wendy, and Nathan.

Kathy holds a B.A. in English Education from Iowa State University but no longer teaches in the school system. She devotes most of her time to leading small-group Bible studies and mentoring other women. Kathy has served as a speaker for women's events and weekend retreats, and she coauthored the book *Facing Choices* while living in the Philippines. She has also written articles for *Discipleship Journal* and other periodicals.